THE HERMITAGE

THE WINTER PALACE
Francesco Bartolommeo Rastrelli

THE SMALL HERMITAGE
Jean-Baptiste Vallin de la Mothe

THE OLD (LARGE) HERMITAGE
Yury Velten

THE RAPHAEL LOGGIAS
Giacomo Quarenghi

THE HERMITAGE THEATRE
Giacomo Quarenghi

THE NEW HERMITAGE
Vasily Stasov and Nikolai Yefimov
to the design by Leo von Klenze

THE HERMITAGE

Buildings and Interiors

"ALFA-COLOUR" · ST PETERSBURG

Introduced by Tatyana Sokolova

Designed by Liubov Rakhmilevich

Translated from the Russian
by Paul Williams

Photographs by Pavel Demidov,
Alexander Kashnitsky,
Leonid Kheifets, Victor Savik,
Vladimir Terebenin and Oleg Trubsky

Printed and bound in Finland
ISBN 5-900959-01-5

The magnificent architectural ensemble which is now the Hermitage was created in two separate periods: the second half of the eighteenth century and the middle of the nineteenth. A wonderful view of all but one of the buildings can be obtained from the Neva.

The Winter Palace, erected between 1754 and 1762 to the design of the famous architect Francesco Bartolommeo Rastrelli (1700—1771), is one of the greatest achievements of the late Russian Baroque. Five other palaces, of more modest dimensions, had been constructed, one after another, before the present Winter Palace came into existence. But hardly anything of them has survived down to the present.

In size and height the Winter Palace dominated its surroundings. But very soon its east front was hidden by the Small Hermitage, a pavilion built adjacent to the Palace between 1764 and 1775. Its architect, Yury Velten, was the Director of the Academy of Fine Arts in St Petersburg; he was also involved in the construction of the granite embankments on the Neva.

The river façade of the Small Hermitage was designed by Jean-Baptiste Vallin de la Mothe, professor of architecture at the Academy. In lightness, simplicity and restraint it is typical of the early Classical period.

The building constructed in 1777—78 on the embankment of the Neva next to the Small Hermitage became known as the Old Hermitage only in the middle of the nineteenth century. This, too, was the work of Velten. It is remarkable for its strict simplicity and is an example of the Classical style without the use of orders.

On the instructions of Catherine II, works of art were acquired for the Hermitage; these were later to become the nucleus of one of the greatest galleries in the world, which has played an important role in the development of Russian culture.

The eighteenth-century ensemble was completed by the Hermitage Theatre, constructed between 1783 and 1787 across the Winter Canal, on the site of the first Winter Palace built for Peter the Great. The architect was Giacomo Quarenghi, a talented Italian who created many beautiful architectural ensembles in Russia. The façade of the theatre is a perfect example of pure eighteenth-century Russian Classicism. The calm magnificence of its structure harmonizes with the three neighbouring buildings (the Winter Palace, the Small Hermitage and the Old Hermitage), making an inimitable whole.

Viewed from Millionnaya Street, the Hermitage buildings have a particular beauty. In the background the silhouette of the Winter Palace is seen against Palace Square, nearer stands the pavilion of the Small Hermitage and, in the foreground, the New Hermitage (1842—1851).

Nikolai Yefimov (1799—1851) and Vasily Stasov (1769—1848) built the New Hermitage to the plan of the Bavarian architect, Leo von Klenze (1784—1864). The building is a clear example of the neo-Greek Classical manner, when architects returned to the legacy of the Ancient World in order to breathe new life into a moribund style.

The most beautiful part of the façade is the entrance — a granite portico charming the eye with the nobility of its proportions. It is decorated with ten huge atlantes carved from monolithic blocks of Serdobol granite in the workshop of Alexander Terebeniov.

The New Hermitage marks a new stage in the history of the museum. The eighteenth-century buildings of the Small Hermitage and the Old Hermitage were used as much for official receptions and amusements as for the accommodation of art collections. The New Hermitage, while remaining part of the palace, was primarily conceived as a museum. It had its own grand staircase and two floors of palatially opulent, yet specifically functional museum halls. The main treasures of the Hermitage were installed here and exhibited for the benefit of a very limited circle of visitors.

The original interiors of the Winter Palace have not survived. They were constantly being rebuilt and redecorated throughout the eighteenth and early nineteenth centuries. All the well-known architects of the period worked on them.

In 1837 the Winter Palace was gutted by a terrible fire which raged for three days and inside the walls only the framework remained. Fortunately the fire did not affect the Small Hermitage or the Old Hermitage.

The Winter Palace was restored very quickly. In less than a year and a half, the decoration of both the exterior and the interior was completed. The work was planned and supervised by Stasov.

The living quarters were redecorated by the architect Alexander Briullov (1798—1877).

It was Stasov who restored the Main Staircase and the Main Palace Church in the same Baroque style in which they had been built by Rastrelli. As for the state rooms -- the Great, Concert, Field Marshals' and Armorial Halls, the Peter the Great Room and others — Stasov successfully gave them the typical features of late Classicism. Traits of eclecticism can be found in the White and Alexander Halls, redecorated by Briullov.

It is interesting to note the technical innovations and special devices used in rebuilding the palace. To avoid another conflagration, stove heating was abolished. The engineer Nikolai Amosov (1787—1868) replaced it by a forced-air heating system. The wood and plaster partitions which had separated the smaller rooms were replaced by brick walls. The small rooms were given vaulted ceilings, whereas the large halls were covered by elaborate metal girders to which were riveted sheets of iron or, as in the case of the St George Hall, copper.

The high technical level reached in the rebuilding of the Winter Palace was sustained in the construction of the New Hermitage.

If we compare the style of the halls of the New Hermitage with those already described, it is apparent that the architect's intention was to create not a palace, but exhibition halls. Nonetheless, the rich splendour of these halls reminds us of the direct link between the museum and the palace.

After the opening of the museum in the 1850s, the rooms of the Old Hermitage were transformed into living quarters. At the same time the Pavilion Hall was built in the Small Hermitage. The work was carried out by Andrei Stakenschneider (1802—1865). One of the capital's leading architects in the middle of the nineteenth century, Stakenschneider was a typical representative of the eclectic school in architecture.

The last significant changes in the palace interiors were made around the turn of the twentieth century by the architects Robert Meltzer (in the Winter Palace) and Leonty Benois (in the foyer of the Hermitage Theatre).

In October 1917 the Winter Palace became the centre of revolutionary events. Following the storming of the palace by Red Guards, soldiers and sailors, the ministers of the Provisional Government were placed under arrest. This event marked advent of a new regime in Russia.

The former royal residence was transferred to the administration of the Hermitage, which became the largest state-owned museum. The main halls of the palace were carefully preserved, while the living quarters and anterooms were gradually adapted for the museum's new exhibits.

During the siege of Leningrad (1941—43) in the Second World War, the Hermitage suffered considerable damage. Dozens of shells pierced the walls of the building, nearby explosions broke nearly every pane of glass. Damp and snow got inside the rooms. Very rare parquet floors were spoiled, paintings darkened and plaster mouldings crumbled.

Restoration began shortly after the lifting of the siege and the art treasures which had been evacuated were gradually returned to their former places. The official reopening of the rooms of the New Hermitage took place on 8 November 1945. Exhibitions were opened one after another in the Small Hermitage, the Old Hermitage and on all the three floors of the Winter Palace.

The majority of the rooms in the Hermitage acquired their present-day appearance between the 1830s and 1860s. One exception in this respect is the interior of the Hermitage Theatre and the adjacent Raphael Loggias which to a certain extent look as they did when created by Quarenghi.

There is no space here to describe all the many interiors and so we shall concentrate on the most interesting.

A visit to the Hermitage usually begins with the central staircase of the Winter Palace. This staircase, created in the eighteenth century by Francesco Bartolommeo Rastrelli, was the setting for the formal reception of foreign envoys and was known as the Ambassadors' Staircase. At Epiphany it came to be used during the traditional Russian Orthodox ceremony of the Blessing of the Waters which was performed on the bank of the Neva and since that ceremony recalls the baptism of Christ in the Jordan, the name of the great biblical river also became attached to the staircase.

The construction of a new throne room — the St George Hall — in the late eighteenth century made it necessary to give a grand appearance to the associated suite of rooms. This was the chief factor behind the design of the Peter the Great Room, the Armorial Hall and the Gallery of the Patriotic War of 1812.

The Peter the Great Room, also known as the Small Throne Room, was created by the architect Auguste Montferrand in 1833 and returned almost entirely to its original appearance when restored by Vasily Stasov after the great fire of 1837. It is extremely richly decorated in a late Classical manner and is devoted to the memory of Peter the Great.

In the niche, a silver throne made in London in 1731 stands on a raised dais. Above the throne is a painting of *Peter the Great and Minerva* produced by the Venetian Jacopo Amigoni in the 1730s.

The Armorial Hall, also restored by Stasov, takes the form of a hall of columns, a type of interior extensively used in Russian Classicism. It gets its name from the coats-of-arms of the Russian provinces which were once displayed on the banners behind the sculptural groups of warriors.

Among the memorials to the military glories of Russian history is the Gallery of the Patriotic War of 1812. It contains 332 portraits of generals who fought to drive Napoleon out of Russia and then pursued him all the way to Paris. The paintings were produced by the English artist George Dawe with the assistance of Russian painters.

The Malachite Room delights visitors with its astonishing combination of vivid colours: an abundance of gold and the bold contrast of the green mineral and crimson upholstery. This was once the main drawing-room in the apartments belonging to Tsar Nicholas I's wife. Now it houses a display of numerous articles made from malachite by Russian craftsmen.

One door of the Malachite Room leads into the Small Dining-room with windows looking onto a small internal courtyard. Light pearly tones are dominant here. On the walls moulded frames imitating shells, scrolls and garlands surround four nineteenth-century tapestries produced in the St Petersburg Factory. This room was decorated by the architect Alexander Briullov who was responsible for several other interiors in the palace, including the magnificent Gold Drawing-room.

The ceiling of this room takes the form of an elaborate vault resting on massive square piers attached to the walls. The entire surface of the walls and piers is gilded so that the delicate ornament almost merges with the wall. Gilded furniture enhances the exceptional impression created.

After visiting several notable rooms of the Winter Palace, we move on now to the already familiar territory of the Small, Old and New Hermitage buildings.

The first room in the Small Hermitage is the Pavilion Hall with a somewhat exotic style of decoration. In devising its complex design the architect Andrei Stakenschneider sought to create a romantic setting in the manner of the East. The hall contains the famous Peacock Clock by the English clockmaker James Cox and also a display of mosaics.

The adjacent Hanging Garden has survived from the eighteenth century. It was constructed on the roof of the palace stables and indoor riding school. The lead sheeting which provided the foundation for the garden was covered with a layer of soil so thick that even today not only flowers but shrubs as well happily grow there. Now marble sculptures are placed amongst the greenery.

From the Small Hermitage a glazed passageway brings us into the Old Hermitage. In the middle of the nineteenth century this building was the venue for sessions of the State Council which were chaired by the Tsar, and therefore we find here the Councillors' Staircase leading down to the Councillors' Entrance, both used by high officials on such occasions.

From the landing of the Councillors' Staircase we have a fine view of the rooms used to display Italian Renaissance art, the most splendid of which is the Leonardo da Vinci Hall. In his design for this interior Stakenschneider borrowed the techniques typical of the seventeenth-century French Baroque. Nowadays the hall is used for the display of two world-famous works by Leonardo — the *Litta Madonna* and the *Benois Madonna.*

The most artistically precious of all the interiors is one created in the eighteenth century. The Raphael Loggias in the Hermitage are a superb copy of the gallery with the same name in the Vatican. The original was designed by Bramante, one of the greatest Renaissance architects, and painted by the great Italian artist Raphael.

Passing through the centre door of the Raphael Loggias we move on to the high vaulted rooms of the New Hermitage, the two Small and one Large Skylight Rooms. With their glazed ceilings and large unbroken expanses of wall, they were intended for the biggest canvases in the collection.

The first Small Skylight Room contains Italian paintings of the sixteenth and seventeenth centuries and items made from lapis lazuli.

The central Large Skylight Room is used to display Italian seventeenth- and eighteenth-century canvases. It is adorned by two malachite vases and four tables with malachite tops as well as four torchères made from porphyry of a splendid violet shade.

The second Small Skylight Room houses works by Spanish sixteenth- and seventeenth-century artists together with two torchères and a bowl of porphyry. All the malachite and prophyry items are richly finished with gilded bronze and rank among the finest examples of Russian lapidary work.

Worthy of special note among the rooms of the New Hermitage is the Knights' Room which contains a display of Western European arms of the fifteenth to eighteenth centuries.

A plain, austere staircase leads down to the lower floor of the New Hermitage. On the upper landing there are vases produced from semi-precious stones by nineteenth-century Russian craftsmen and also works by Italian sculptors.

The large halls on the lower floor are attractive for the plain simplicity of their decoration. They were obviously designed as part of a museum. Here we find the art of the Ancient World represented by white marble sculptures. In order to create the best viewing conditions the walls here are faced with artificial marble of various colours — red, greyish-green and pinkish-lilac.

The Hall of Dionysius contains the most celebrated statue in the Hermitage — the Tauride Venus dating from the third century B.C.

In terms of architectural composition the Hall of Twenty Columns is the most successful in the New Hermitage. It was designed to house a display of classical painted vases and the architect, Leo von Klenze, employed a number of devices adopted from his Ancient Greek predecessors.

Two rows of grey columns divide the hall into two aisles and a narrower central nave. This way of dividing the interior was customary in Greek and Roman temples. The corner room on the lower

floor is reminiscent of the atrium in a Graeco-Roman house. Such inner courtyards usually had a fountain in the middle and here we see an ancient fountain sculpture depicting Aura, the goddess of the morning breeze, riding on a swan.

The attraction of one of the rooms on the lower floor lies not in its decor but in an immense stone bowl, large and tall enough for a group of people to stand beneath it. This is the Kolyvan Vase which was carved from an immense block of Altai jasper weighing almost eleven and a half tonnes.

Apart from its uniquely decorated halls, the New Hermitage has less opulent rooms which nevertheless attract a constant stream of visitors. They house the display of Dutch and Flemish painting, the most popular parts of which are the rooms containing the works by the Small Dutch Masters, Rembrandt, Snyders, Rubens and Van Dyck.

The Hermitage Theatre lies beyond the Old Hermitage building. A large foyer with a festive atmosphere was constructed in the area connecting the two. At the present time this foyer is frequently used for temporary exhibitions.

A noble simplicity is the distinguishing characteristic of the remarkable theatre auditorium created by Giacomo Quarenghi and Carlo Rossi. On entering a member of the audience would not see the customary tiers of ornately decorated boxes rising upwards, but steps going down and benches arranged in a series of semicircles like an amphitheatre. Today performances and concerts are once again being given in the Hermitage Theatre.

The Hermitage is a magnificent treasure-house of culture and art. All the buildings and interiors of the Hermitage with their splendid architecture and decor are of great artistic value and a fitting memorial to the work of the architects and craftsmen, painters and sculptors.

At present the Hermitage possesses over two and a half million works of art, including some 15,000 paintings, over 12,000 sculptures, more than 600,000 prints and drawings, and about 1,000,000 coins and medals. Among the great artists whose works can be found here are Leonardo da Vinci, Raphael, Michelangelo, Titian, Veronese, Rembrandt, Rubens, Watteau, Renoir, Picasso and Matisse.

Illustrations

2

The garden in front of the western façade of the Winter Palace

3
The Jordan (Ambassadors') Staircase
Architects FRANCESCO BARTOLOMMEO RASTRELLI, 1753–59; VASILY STASOV, 1837–39

6
Decorative vase. 1825—50
Russia, St Petersburg. The Imperial Glassworks
Ruby-coloured and colourless crystal, faceted,
in ormolu mount. Height 56 cm

7

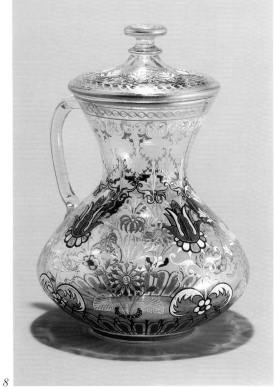

8

10

11

7
Decanter, goblet and wineglass. 18th century.
Russia
Glass, engraving

8
Jug. 1800–50
Russia, St Petersburg.
The Imperial Glassworks.
Glass, painted in enamel
colours. Height 23 cm

9
Goblet. 1700–25
Russia. The Yamburg
Glassworks.
Colourless glass, with
engraved decoration.
Height 20 cm

10
Vessel for claret-cup.
1896–1908. Russia, Moscow.
The Ovchinnikov Factory.
Silver, embossed, with filigree,
enamel and gilt decoration.
Height 20 cm

11
The Crucifixion.
Central part of the icon
with marginal scenes.
11th or 12th century.
Byzantium
Silver, chased, with *cloisonné*
enamel decoration

The Peter the Great, or Small Throne, Room
Architects Auguste Montferrand, 1833; Vasily Stasov, 1837–38

13
Silver throne
of Empress Anna Ioannovna. 1731
London. By Nicholas Clausen

15
JEAN-MARC NATTIER. 1685–1766
France
PORTRAIT OF PETER I. 1717
Oil on canvas. 142.5 x 110 cm

WINTER PALACE

16
The Concert Hall. Decorative sculptures

19 →
Vase. 1840s
Russia. Peterhof Lapidary Works
Malachite, gilt bronze. Height 68 cm

18 →
Articles made of malachite. 1800–50
Russia. Peterhof Lapidary Works

18

19

22
The Gold Drawing-room
Architect ALEXANDER BRIULLOV, 1839

23

24

23
Cameo: *The Adoration of the Shepherds.*
Late 16th century
Italy, Milan. The circle of ALESSANDRO MASNAGO
Agate. 4.5 x 4.9 cm

24
Cameo: *Mars and Venus.* 1530s
France
Shell. 7.8 x 6.5 cm (without mount)

25

25
Cameo: *Ptolemy II and Arsinoë*
(The Gonzaga Cameo). 3rd century B.C.
Alexandria (?)
Three-layered sardonyx. 15.7 x 11.8 cm

26
Cameo: *Joseph and His Brothers.* Ca 1240
Southern Italy
Sardonyx. 5.4 x 6.5 cm (without mount)

27
Cameo: *Zeus.* 3rd century B.C.
Alexandria
Sardonyx. Diameter 6.1 cm

26

27

29
Boudoir
Architects Alexander Briullov, 1839; Harald Bosse, 1853

The Green Dining-room
Architect ALEXANDER BRIULLOV, 1860s

31
Intaglio: *Medusa.* 5th century B.C.
Chalcedony, gold. 2.9 x 2.3 cm

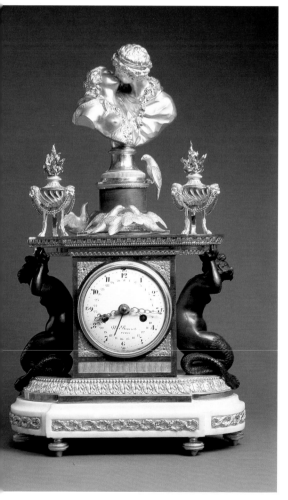

33
Candelabrum for two candles.
Mid-18th century
Russia, St Petersburg.
The Imperial Porcelain Factory
Porcelain, ormolu. 40 x 36 x 15 cm

32
Mantel clock. 1780s
France, Paris
After the model by JEAN-ANTOINE HOUDON
Ormolu. 54 x 27 x 14 cm

34
Intaglio: *Alexander the Great
in the Guise of Zeus.*
4th — 3rd century B.C.
Cornelian. 3 x 2.1 cm

38

GEORGE DAWE. 1781—1829. England
PORTRAIT OF GENERAL
PIOTR BAGRATION. Ca 1823
Oil on canvas. 70 x 62.5 cm

39

GEORGE DAWE. 1781—1829. England
PORTRAIT OF GENERAL
NIKOLAI RAYEVSKY
Oil on canvas. 70 x 62.5 cm

40

GEORGE DAWE. 1781—1829. England
PORTRAIT OF GENERAL
ALEXANDER TUCHKOV
Oil on canvas. 70 x 62.5 cm

38

39

40

The Gallery of the Patriotic War of 1812
Architects CARLO ROSSI, 1826; VASILY STASOV, 1839

42

JOSHUA REYNOLDS. 1723–1792. England
CUPID UNTYING THE GIRDLE OF VENUS. 1788
Oil on canvas. 127.5 x 101 cm

42

43

44

43

THOMAS GAINSBOROUGH. 1727–1788. England
PORTRAIT OF A LADY IN BLUE. Late 1770s
Oil on canvas. 76 x 64 cm

44

GEORGE MORLAND. 1763–1804. England
THE APPROACHING STORM. 1791
Oil on canvas. 85 x 117 cm

45

46

45

LUCAS CRANACH THE ELDER. 1472–1553. Germany
PORTRAIT OF A WOMAN
Oil on panel. 88.5 x 58.6 cm

46

GEORG FLEGEL. 1566–1638. Germany
STILL LIFE WITH FLOWERS AND FOOD
Oil on panel. 52.5 x 41 cm

47

AMBROSIUS HOLBEIN. Ca 1495 – ca 1519. Germany
PORTRAIT OF A YOUNG MAN
Oil on panel. 44 x 32.5 cm

47

48
Cabinet. 1650–1700
France. Decorated by ANTOINE LEPAUTRE
Ebony, ivory, tortoise-shell

48

50

49
Armchair. Mid-18th century
France. By ETIENNE DIEUDONNÉ
Wood, carved, gilded and upholstered
with tapestry. 97 x 65 x 52 cm

49

50

Commode. 1765—70
Germany. By ABRAHAM ROENTGEN (1711—1793)
and DAVID ROENTGEN (1743—1807)
Wood, inlay of contrasting wood, with bronze mounts.
87 x 103 x 56 cm

51

Wardrobe. 1650—1700
France, Paris. By ANDRÉ-CHARLES BOULLE (1642—1732)
Ebony, with ormolu mounts and marquetry decorations.
255 x 170 x 64 cm

52

Commode. Mid-18th century
Italy, Venice
Wood, with painted decoration and ormolu mounts.
82 x 120 x 58 cm

52

53

Secretaire. Ca 1760
France, Paris. By JEAN-FRANÇOIS DUBUT (?—1778)
Rosewood, with ivory and mother-of-pearl decorations
and ormolu mounts. 144 x 111 x 48 cm

51

53

The enfilade of rooms housing the display of 18th-century French art
Architect ALEXANDER BRIULLOV, 1839

55
The enfilade of rooms housing the display of 18th-century French art
Architect ALEXANDER BRIULLOV, 1839

56
Jean-Antoine Houdon. 1741–1828. France
Voltaire
Marble. Height 138 cm

57
Etienne-Maurice Falconet. 1716–1791. France
Winter. 1771
Marble. Height 140 cm

56

57

58
Jean-Marc Nattier. 1685–1766. France
Portrait of a Lady in Grey
Oil on canvas. 80 x 64 cm

59
Antoine Watteau. 1684–1721. France
A Capricious Woman. Ca 1718
Oil on canvas. 42 x 34 cm

60
FRANÇOIS BOUCHER. 1703–1770. France
PASTORAL SCENE
Oil on canvas. 61 x 75 cm

60

58

59

61

61
JEAN-BAPTISTE GREUZE. 1725–1805. France
HEAD OF A GIRL IN A CAP. 1760s
Oil on canvas. 41 x 33 cm

Bureau. 1785. Germany. By Dᴀᴠɪᴅ Rᴏᴇɴᴛɢᴇɴ (1743–1807)
Mahogany and oak, with ormolu and brass mounts. 119 x 141 x 87 cm

The Gothic Library
Architect ALEXANDER KRASOVSKY, 1890s

65
Book binding. 19th century. England
Leather, gold stamping. 18.7 x 13.4 cm

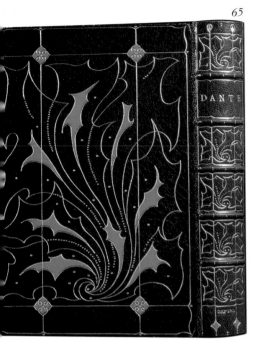

66
Book binding. 16th century. Italy
Leather, gold stamping. 22.5 x 15.5 cm

67
Rider and His Retinue. 1625—50
India. Mogul School
Miniature on paper. 37 x 28 cm

68
Book binding. 18th century. Germany
Velvet, silver. 17 x 11 cm

The Small Hermitage. The northern pavilion
Architect Jean-Baptiste Vallin de la Mothe, 1767—69

SMALL HERMITAGE

70
The Hanging Garden
Architect VASILY STASOV, 1840–44

The Pavilion Hall. The Peacock Clock. 18th century
England. By JAMES COX

The Pavilion Hall. Part of the interior

75
The Old (Large) Hermitage
Architect Yury Velten, 1771−87

76
The Councillors' Staircase. The upper landing

OLD HERMITAGE

78
WORKSHOP OF ANDREA DELLA ROBBIA.
15th — early 16th century. Italy
Relief: *Madonna and Child*
Majolica. Height 128 cm

The Leonardo da Vinci Hall
Architect ANDREI STAKENSCHNEIDER, 1858

81
LEONARDO DA VINCI. 1452–1519. Italy
MADONNA WITH A FLOWER (THE BENOIS MADONNA)
Oil on canvas (transferred from panel). 49.5 x 31.5 cm

85
The foyer of the theatre
Architect LEONTY BENOIS, 1904

86
The auditorium
Architect GIACOMO QUARENGHI, 1786–87

View of the Winter Canal and the New Hermitage

New Hermitage

New Hermitage

The New Hermitage. The southern façade
The decor of a window opening

The State Staircase. Architects Vasily Stasov
and Nikolai Yefimov to the design by Leo von Klenze, 1842–51

94
Gold earring from a barrow near Theodosia.
4th century B.C.

95
*Amphora from the Chertomlyk Barrow
(the Lower Dnieper Basin).* 4th century B.C.
Silver, engraved and chased, parcel-gilt. Height 70 cm

96

98

97

96
*Vessel from the Solokha Barrow
(the Dnieper Basin).* 4th century B.C.
Gold. Height 13 cm

97
Guhyapati. 18th century
Tibet
Gilded bronze. Height 24 cm

98
Dish. 7th–8th century
Iran
Parcel-gilt silver. Diameter 28 cm

NEW HERMITAGE

99
The Swan Room. Architects VASILY STASOV
and NIKOLAI YEFIMOV to the design by LEO VON KLENZE, 1842–51

The Athena Room. Architects VASILY STASOV
and NIKOLAI YEFIMOV to the design by LEO VON KLENZE, 1842–51

New Hermitage

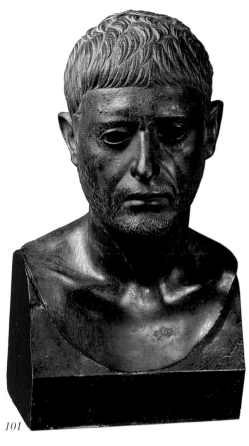

101

101
Portrait of a Roman.
75–100 B.C. Rome
Bronze. Height 39 cm

102
*Portrait of Emperor
Balbinus.* 225–250. Rome
White (Carrara) marble.
Height 72.5 cm

102

104, 106
The Hall of Twenty Columns. Architects Vasily Stasov
and Nikolai Yefimov to the design by Leo von Klenze, 1842−51

105
Pelike: *The First Swallow.* Ca 510 B.C.
Greece, Attica. Workshop of Euphronios
Pottery. Height 37.5 cm

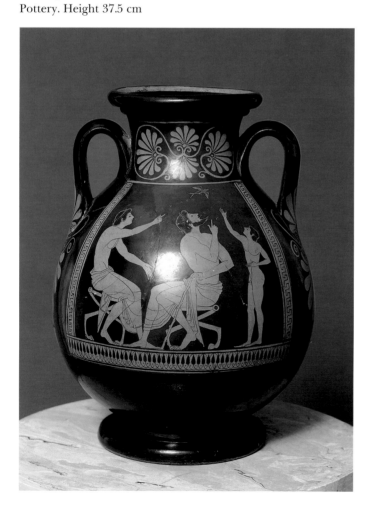

New Hermitage

107
*Medal commemorating Peter I's first journey
abroad in 1697—98*
Saxony. By CHRISTIAN WERMUTH
Silver. Diameter 6.2 cm

109, 110
*Medal commemorating the conclusion of the Peace
of Nystad, 30 August 1721* (obverse and reverse)
Russia
Gold. Diameter 6 cm

108
*Medal commemorating Peter I's visit
to the Paris Mint.* 1717
Paris. By JEAN DU VIVIER and MICHAEL ROEG
Silver. Diameter 6 cm

The Hall of Twelve Columns (The Coin Hall). Architects Vasily Stasov and Nikolai Yefimov to the design by Leo von Klenze, 1842−51

112

The Large Skylight Room. Architects VASILY STASOV
and NIKOLAI YEFIMOV to the design by LEO VON KLENZE, 1842–51

113
Small Skylight Room. Architects VASILY STASOV
and NIKOLAI YEFIMOV to the design by LEO VON KLENZE, 1842–51

114
EL GRECO. 1541—1614. Spain
THE APOSTLES PETER AND PAUL.
Between 1587 and 1592
Oil on canvas. 121.5 x 105 cm

115
TINTORETTO. 1518—1594. Italy
THE BIRTH OF JOHN THE BAPTIST. Ca 1550
Oil on canvas. 181 x 266 cm

116
CARAVAGGIO. 1571—1610. Italy
THE LUTE-PLAYER. Ca 1595
Oil on canvas. 94 x 119 cm

114

115

116

The Gallery of the History of Ancient Painting. Architects VASILY STASOV
and NIKOLAI YEFIMOV to the design by LEO VON KLENZE, 1842—51

119

ANTONIO CANOVA. 1757—1822. Italy
THE THREE GRACES. Marble. Height 180 cm

120
Vase. 1830s–1840s. Russia
Malachite. Height 99 cm

121
REMBRANDT HARMENSZ VAN RIJN.
1606–1669. Holland
FLORA. 1664
Oil on canvas. 125 x 101 cm

122
REMBRANDT HARMENSZ VAN RIJN.
1606–1669. Holland
DAVID AND URIAH. Ca 1665
Oil on canvas. 127 x 116 cm

123

124

123
WILLEM CLAESZ HEDA. 1594−1680/82
Holland
BREAKFAST WITH LOBSTER. 1648
Oil on canvas. 118 x 118 cm

125
Tent-roofed Room (Room of Dutch Painting). Architects Vasily Stasov
and Nikolai Yefimov to the design by Leo von Klenze, 1842—51

124
Pieter de Hooch. 1629 — after 1684
Holland
Mistress and Maid. Ca 1660
Oil on canvas. 53 x 42 cm

126

127

126
Rogier van der Weyden.
Ca 1400—1464
The Netherlands
St Luke Drawing the Virgin
Oil on canvas (transferred from panel)
102.5 x 108.5 cm

127
Gerard David. Ca 1460—1523
The Netherlands
*The Virgin Embracing
the Dead Christ*
Oil on panel. 36 x 44.5 cm

128
Jacob Jordaens. 1593–1678
Flanders
The Bean King. 1638
Oil on canvas. 157 x 211 cm

129
Frans Snyders. 1579–1657
Flanders
Fish Shop
Oil on canvas. 209.5 x 341 cm

128

129

The Snyders Room (Room of Flemish Painting)
Architects VASILY STASOV and NIKOLAI YEFIMOV to the design by LEO VON KLENZE, 1842–51

131
FRANS SNYDERS. 1579—1657. Flanders
*BOWL OF FRUIT ON A RED
TABLE-CLOTH*
Oil on canvas. 59.8 x 90.8 cm

PETER PAUL RUBENS. 1577–1640. Flanders
THE UNION OF EARTH AND WATER. Ca 1618
Oil on canvas. 222.5 x 180.5 cm

133

134

133
PETER PAUL RUBENS.
1577–1640. Flanders
ROMAN CHARITY. Ca 1612
Oil on canvas. 140.5 x 180.3 cm

134
PETER PAUL RUBENS.
1577–1640. Flanders
*PERSEUS AND
ANDROMEDA.* 1620s
Oil on canvas. 99.5 x 139 cm

135
Anthony van Dyck. 1599—1641. Flanders
Portrait of Philadelphia and Elizabeth
Wharton. 1630s
Oil on canvas. 162 x 130 cm

136
The Van Dyck Room. Architects VASILY STASOV
and NIKOLAI YEFIMOV to the design by LEO VON KLENZE, 1842–51

137
The Knights' Room. Architects VASILY STASOV
and NIKOLAI YEFIMOV to the design by LEO VON KLENZE, 1842–51

138
The Knights' Room. Part of display

139
A scudello plate. Ca 1550. Italy, Urbino
Majolica, with painted decoration. Diameter 20.5 cm

140
An apothecary's vessel. Early 16th century. Italy
Majolica. Height 40 cm

142
Cassone with fantastic sea creatures.
1550–1600. Italy, Florence
Carved wood. 54 x 165 x 61 cm

143
MICHELANGELO BUONARROTI. 1475–1564. Italy
CROUCHING BOY. Ca 1524
Marble. Height 54 cm

144
RAPHAEL SANTI. 1483–1520. Italy
THE CONESTABILE MADONNA. 1502–03
Tempera on canvas (transferred from panel).
17.5 x 18 cm

The Italian Majolica Room. Detail of ceiling painting

Здания и залы Эрмитажа

Альбом (на английском языке)

ТОО «АЛЬФА-КОЛОР». Санкт-Петербург. 1997
ЛР № 063313, 28 февраля 1994

Цветоделение и диапозитивы изготовлены
фирмой «AMOS», Санкт-Петербург

Набор, верстка текста, изготовление черно-белых
диапозитивов – «Аврора-Дизайн», Санкт-Петербург

PRINTED AND BOUND IN FINLAND